AN ARTIST'S VIEW OF THE TIDE MILL AT WOODBRIDGE

BY

David Green

Greensprings Press, Woodbridge

To Peter Cropper

ISBN 978 09533681 81
greenspringspress@googlemail.com
Printed by Bettaprint Woodbridge Limited
First published 2010

THE COLOUR PLATES

PREFACE

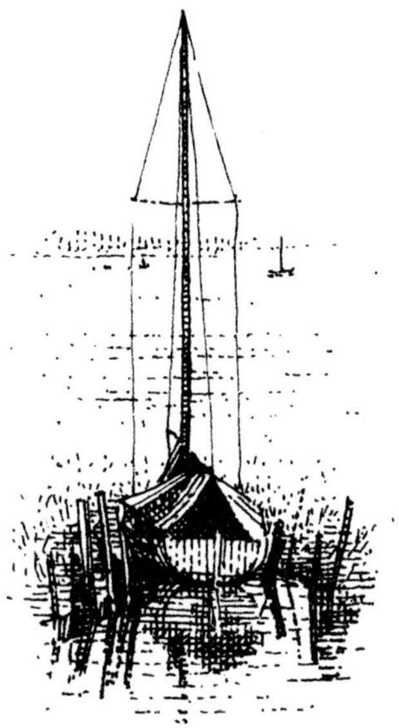

I first became aware of the Tide Mill at Woodbridge when I was called upon to draw some maps for a book on the subject of the Historic Towns of East Anglia by David Lloyd and published in 1989 by Gollancz in association with my friend Peter Crawley. There in those pages the waterfront at Woodbridge is given a full double page illustration with the Tide Mill freshly restored and sparkling so brightly in the sun in contrast to everything else about that I suspect it marginally upset the balance in the exposure meter of the camera, leaving the remainder of the scene – the water, the boats, the harbour buildings and the trees on the far bank-underexposed and too dark.

Then a year or two later one of those periodic financial crises hit the country and my wife and I were forced to move out of our house in Bath. In the event we were rescued by the generosity of a cousin who had just bought a retirement bungalow and was prepared to wait a while before moving in. It was in Woodbridge.

How much more fortunate could we have been? From the moment we arrived I was enchanted by the town, the river and indeed the whole of the East Anglian Coastal scene which has provided virtually all the subject matter for my paintings ever since.

A glance will reveal that my viewpoint is straightforward, but much is perceived beneath the surface, differentiating – consciously and unconsciously – the views chosen for painting from their surroundings. This process of elimination is highly personal, entirely traditional and it soon connects with the abstract nature of picture making. Merely topographical images have no interest for me and neither do those that have no basis in anything that has not been observed and enjoyed.

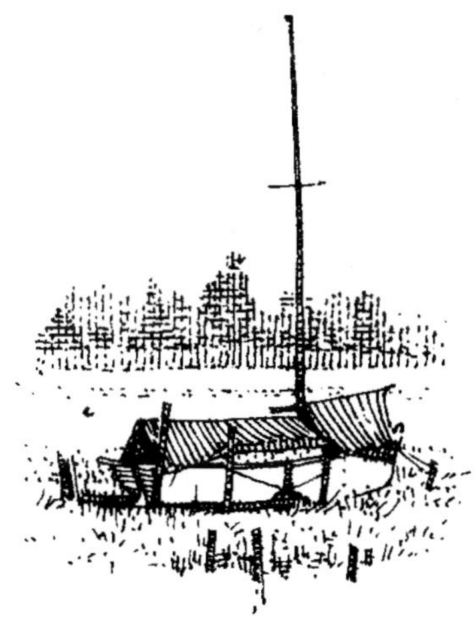

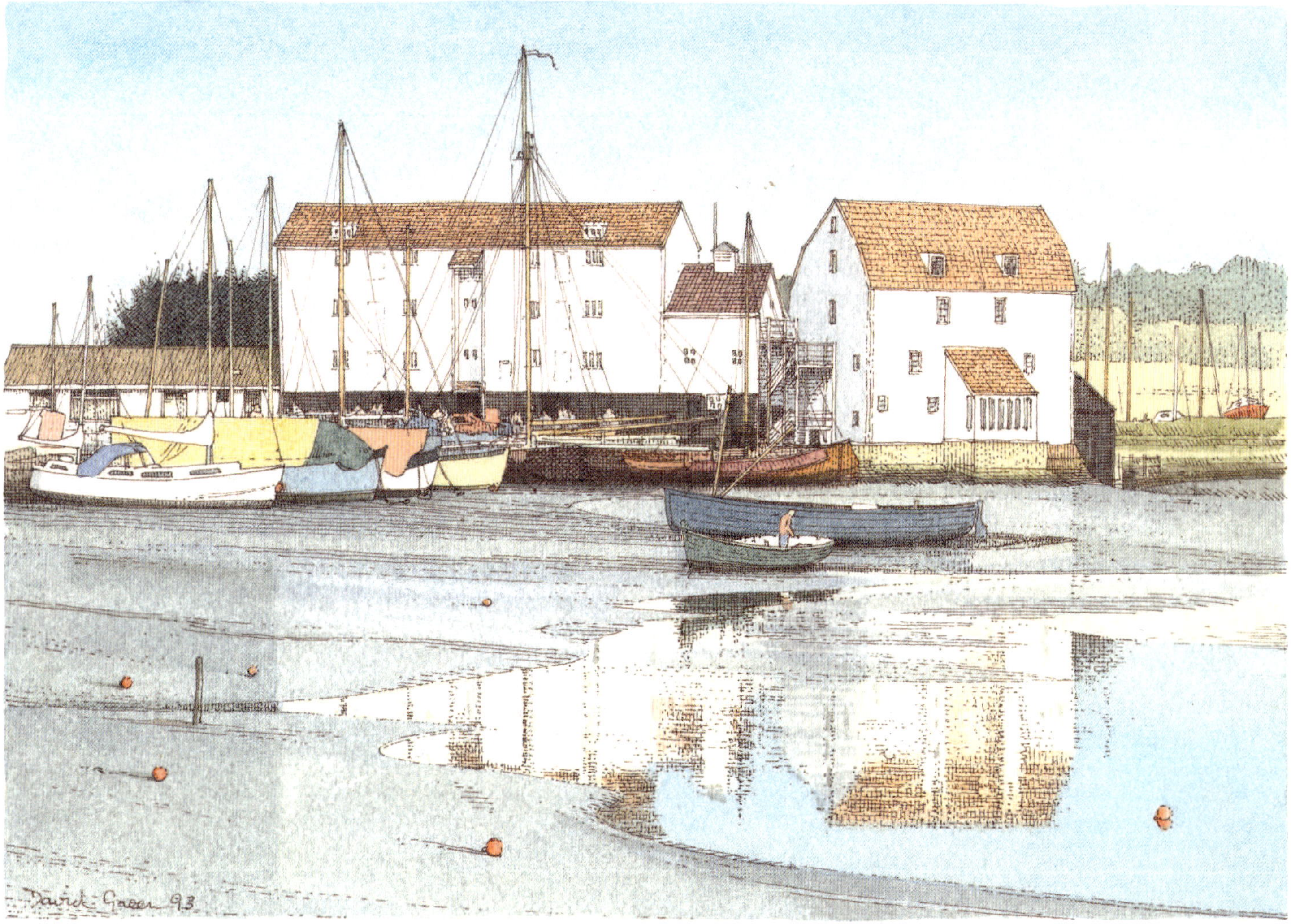

Plate One THE GRANARY, THE COTTAGE AND THE TIDE MILL

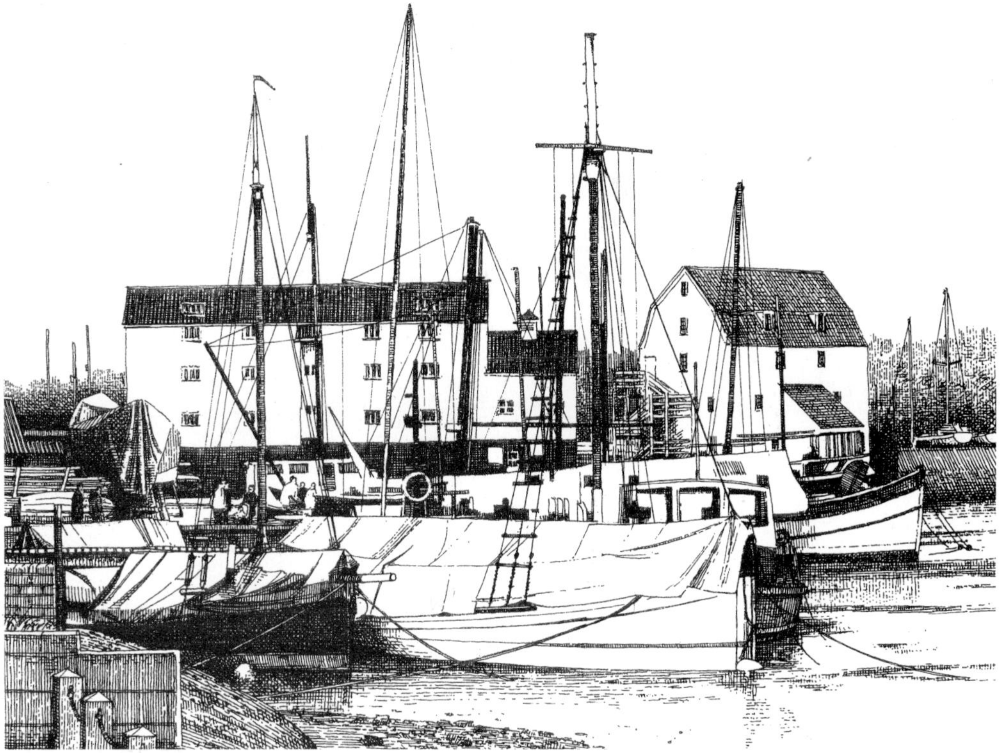

From the Dock

HAVE YOU EVER visited the Tide Mill at Woodbridge? In an age of such high levels of consciousness of fuel and energy conservation it represents a truly magnificent achievement of which Woodbridge is justly proud and which is well explained in the Mill itself by models, diagrams and an excellent historical booklet. No comparable tide mill exists anywhere within these shores. The present building has stood here for over two hundred years and it is known that other mills have occupied this site for at least six hundred years before that.

And what a site! It juts out across the River Deben at an angle that allowed the Mill to be built facing due south to the sun, but there was not enough room there to build a sufficiently capacious grain store next door to it or even on quite the same line. So the two buildings that were eventually put up face the sun differently and here

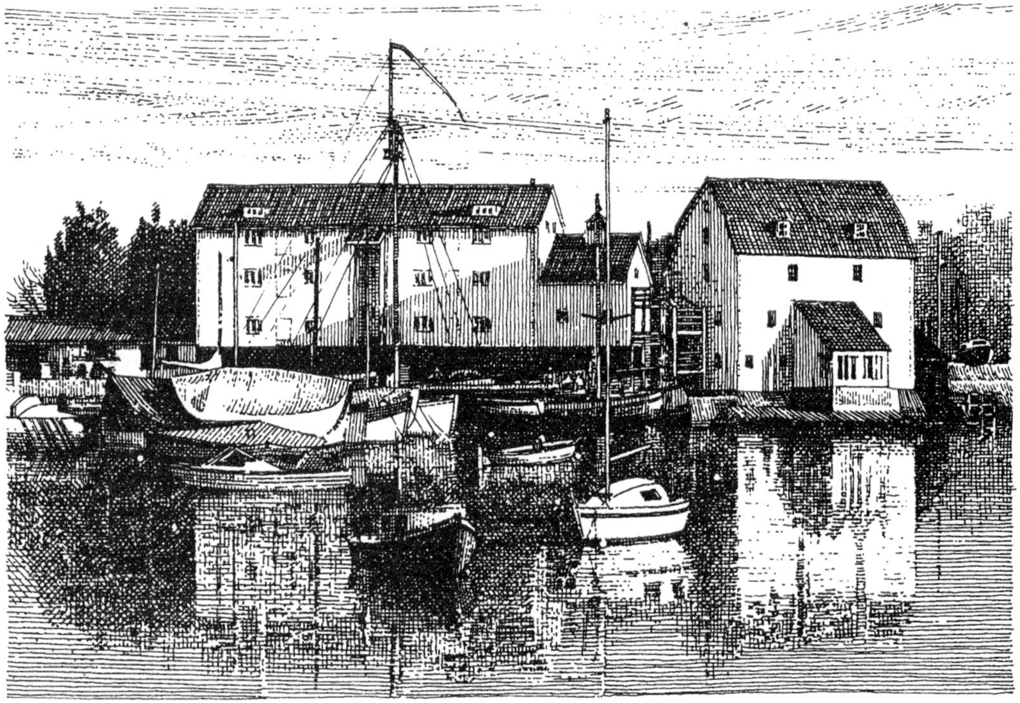

Soon after 11am

begins the visual element of their fascination for the light and shadow swaps about between them at almost every hour of the day. First one is in full sun, the other in shadow; then the light moves steadily across until the picture is reversed. At one point only the end of the Granary is lit; at another only the west end of the Mill and so it goes on until the sun begins to fade leaving both buildings glowing with stored luminous energy against a darkening background of trees and the river.

The Mill was working until 1957 when the main shaft broke. From then it slowly decayed until a rescue operation was set in motion through the foresight and generosity of a Mrs Gardener who bought both the Mill and the Granary in 1968 after listening to a revealing lecture on their significance by the local historian Norman Scarfe.

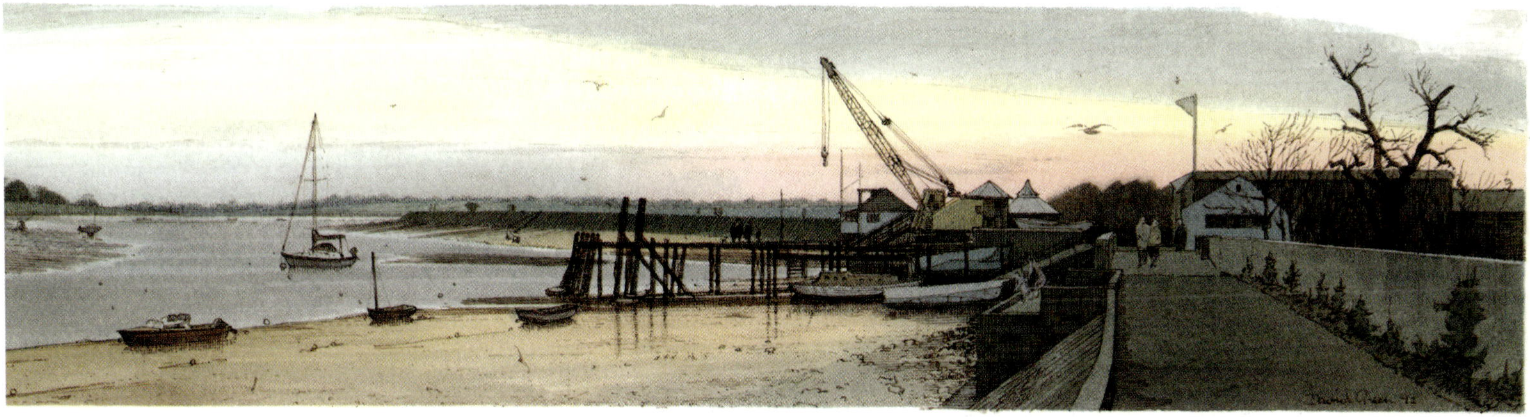

Plate Two. *SUNDOWN, LOOKING SOUTH*

Restoration began with the Mill. On the cover of the present guide to the Mill is a splendid photograph showing it fully restored and gleeming in full sun beside the derelict Granary still sheathed in the rusting corrugated iron which had covered, and very likely preserved, both buildings from the beginning of that century.

Conversion of the Granary into six flats was commenced around 1990 and people were living there by 1993. The conversion was sensitively done. The original central hoist was replaced by a false one which casts a diagonal shadow across the buildings during the latter part of the morning, before the sun has moved round to light up the whole facade. The building is also set formally upon a black tarred base which provides a strong visual foundation as well as protection against high tides which occasionally flood across the Quay.

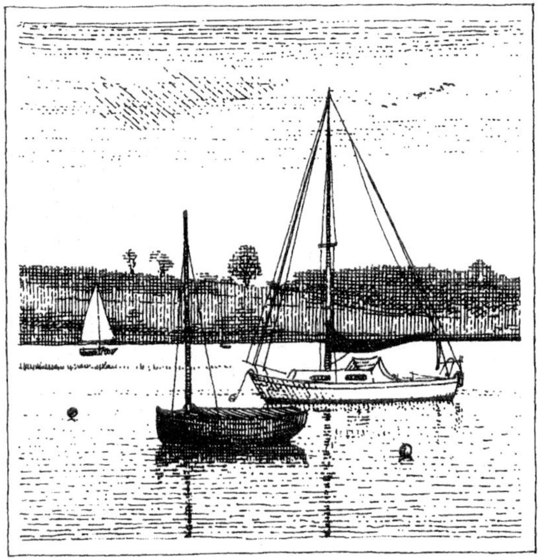

Across the river

Tucked onto the eastern end of the Granary is a smaller building which was converted into a cottage. It soon becomes apparent that this seemingly insignificant structure is in fact a key to the harmony of the entire Quay complex for its roof, with its lesser height, darker colour and delightful ventilator, is perfectly placed to break up the potential monotony of two long weatherboarded facades. Without this break the visual pleasure of the two main buildings would be lost and it would only be the ecological function of the Tide Mill, rather than its aesthetic beauty as part of a varied complex of buildings, that could evoke public interest.

Perhaps this might seem to be rather overstating the case, but taking a ruler to a frontal photograph of the whole facade it soon becomes apparent that the Cottage is not only a key element visually, but is also a key element mathematically. The Mill looked at square on is twice as long as the Cottage and the Granary is four times. Further, the end of the Cottage – either fully lit in the morning sun or in the dark shadow later in the day – is at a critical measure known in the mathematical world or any creative design studio as the Divine Proportion or Golden Mean. In actual measurements this mystical division is two fifths to three fifths (or more accurately 0.617 to 0.383), but anyone

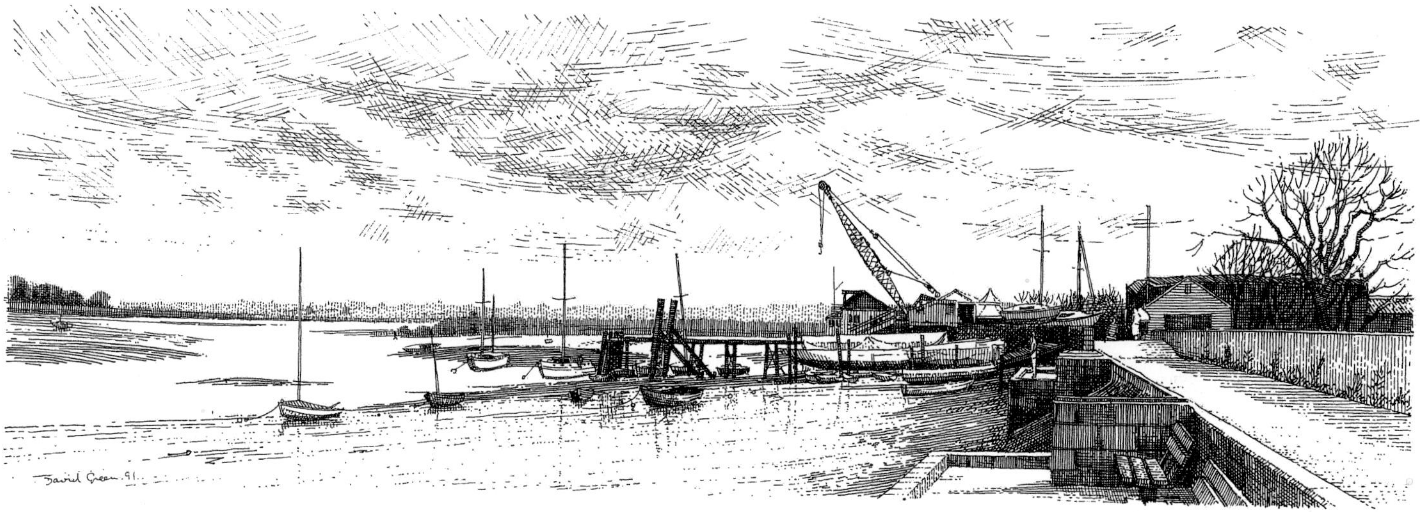

Eversons' Crane

seeking a fuller explanation of the true significance of this division will soon be lost in the intellectual world of the ancient Greeks and the theories of Euclid, Mascheroni, Fibonacci and the world of pentagons, polyhedrons, reciprocal rectangles et al. So, bye for now!

THE DIVINE PROPORTION OR GOLDEN MEAN: the most satisfying division of a line, a space or a volume into two unequal parts used instinctively by artists from all periods, races and in all media. The division works both horizontally and vertically in either direction as shown here.

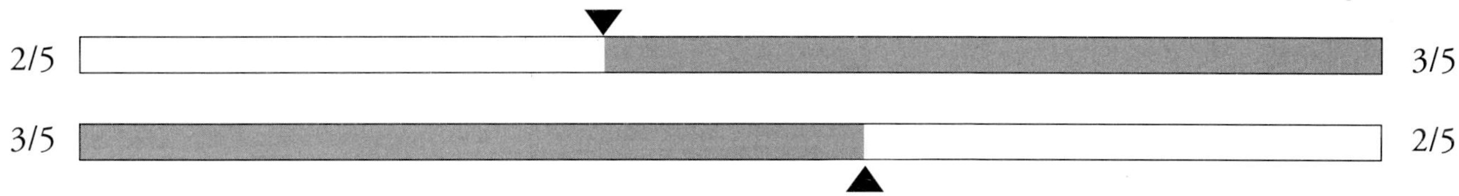

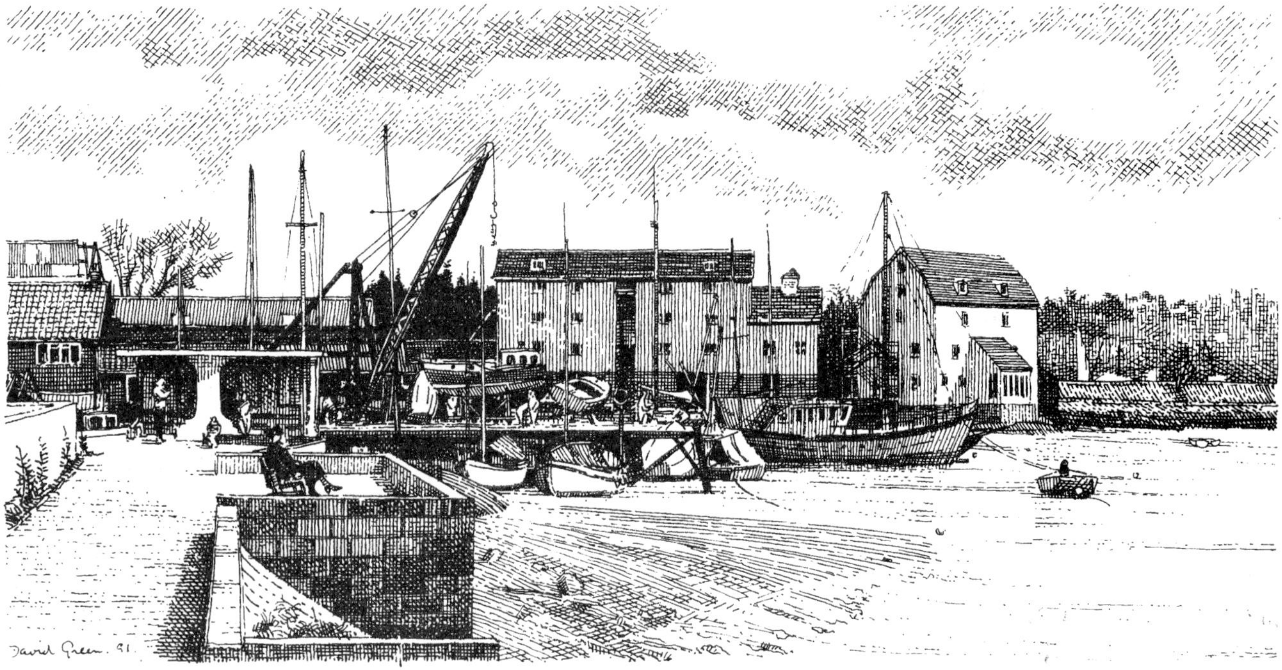

From the River Walk

The fact is of course that in terms of architectural design such mathematical concepts grip our attention without us realising. Three dimensional forms or two dimensional shapes, based firmly on the mathematical harmony of proportions, will always command attention.

But can we be sure that the placing of the Tide Mill and the Granary was in fact planned with such care and deliberation? Either way because things have turned out so well on Woodbridge Quay, we have a complex of buildings that is infinitely pleasing to the eye. It could so easily have turned out differently and then we should have been faced with just another mill, another grain store and a caretaker's cottage which no one would think twice about or even notice.

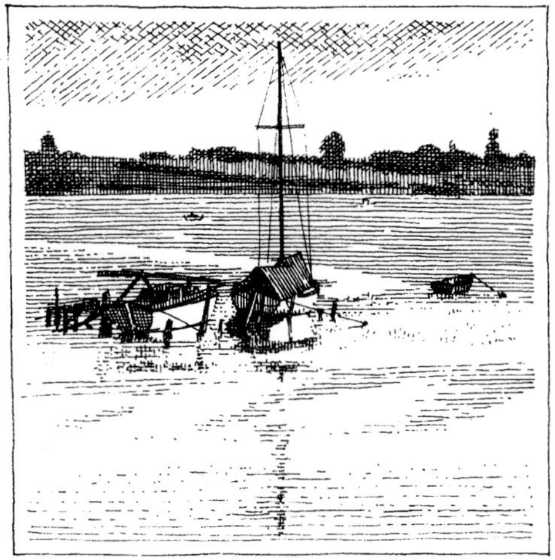

At Kyson Point

The daily cycle of light and shadow across the faces of these buildings and their geometrical proportions, is however only half the attraction of this marvellous Quayside. There is also the twice daily exchange between the mud and the water in the lower half of the scene caused by the tide. This results in constantly changing shapes in the reflections of the Mill, the Granary, the boats, the buoys and the passers by. No two views of this scene are ever quite the same and one can always return to it confident that there will be a fresh miracle to satisfy your mind and to please your visual consciousness.

* * * * *

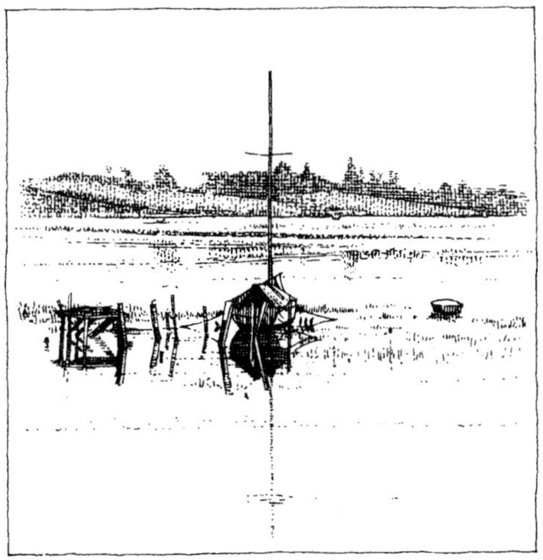

Low Tide

As soon as I turned the corner from The Avenue and started to walk along the river path towards the Mill on the sunny day recorded on page six I was spellbound. All the breath left my body in one gasp and the hairs on the back of my neck tingled with excitement. Here indeed was something uniquely special, a view that positively had to be recorded to share with everyone who enjoys the best of what Woodbridge has to offer. And it was not just the Mill, it was the whole of the Quayside scene – the Mill, the Cottage, the Granary, the boats, the river and the reflections enclosed so dramatically within the remains of the receding tide.

I was thrilled too by the dazzling brilliance of the white weatherboarding in full sun and the stark contrast of the tarred basement of the Granary, together with the other dark shapes – the conifers and the wheelhouse – which appeared like bookends keeping the buildings pressed together. Then, to complete the picture there were the lovely colours of the roofs and the tarpaulins stretched over the boats, contrasting so gently with the quiet grey of the mud and the pale cloudless sky.

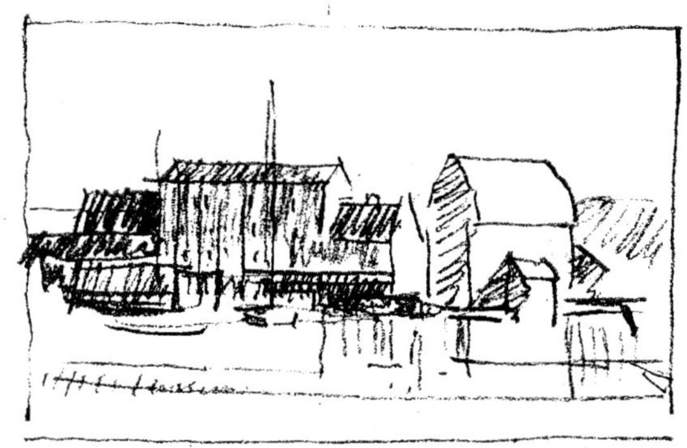

Preliminary notes

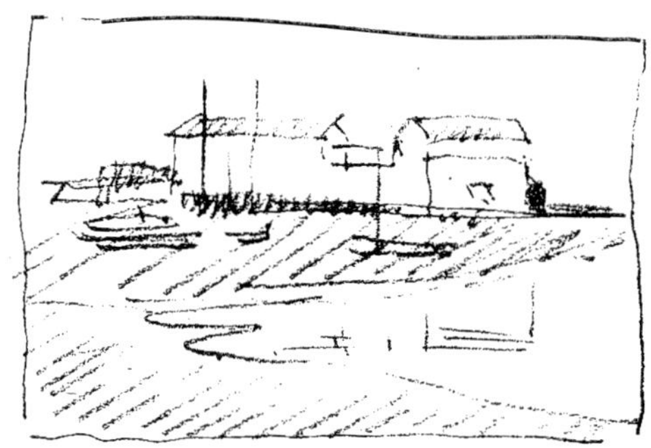

Yes, a picture indeed and a scene no longer to be looked at as a collection of separate buildings, no matter how well they sit together in harmonious proportions, or how lovely each is on its own. There are now distinctive sky shapes above them, a foreground showing below and definite limits at either side which contribute just as much to the end result as the abstract geometry of the buildings themselves. Where should these limits be set and just how big is the final drawing or painting to be?

Size is of course conditioned by factors such as the paper, the canvas or indeed the wall if a mural is in mind, as well as the artist's vision. But the comfortable placing of the objects – the Mill, the Granary, the Cottage etc. within the

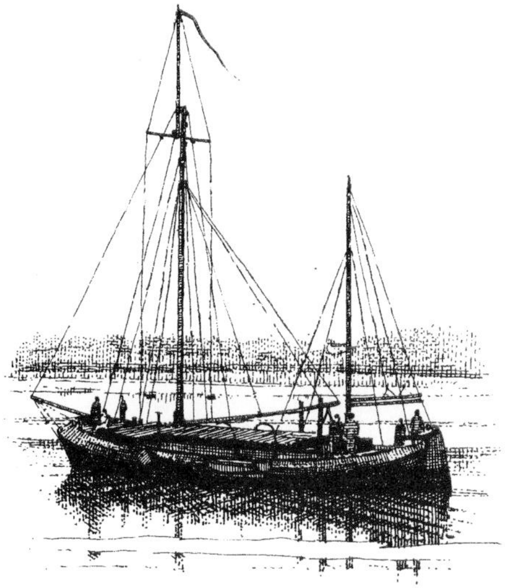

Neljan

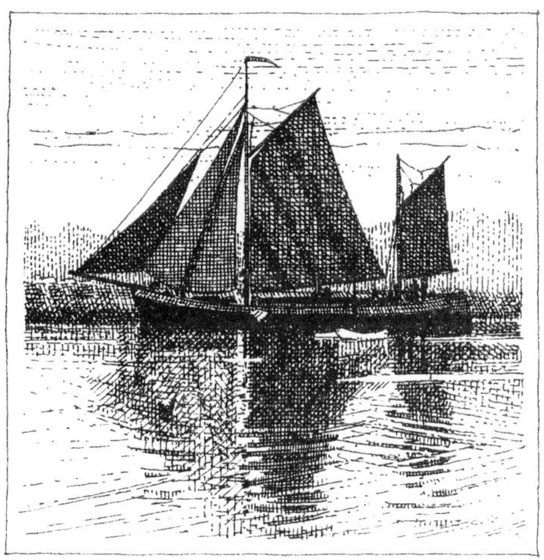

Neljan under sail

chosen area is highly critical and it has everything to do with the appeal of the end result. Just where should the scene be cut off at the bottom, how much space is needed on either side of the buildings and how far should one extend the sky?

At the bottom there is a very clear indication of the placing in the grand sweep into the picture from the water's edge on the right. The inward sweep suggests an appropriate placing of the bottom right hand corner and therefore also defines the right hand side of the frame. This vertical cut off includes in the picture just sufficient of the far bank and the distant landscape on the right to serve as a background to the Mill and to balance with what needs to be included on the far left, namely the low Art Club building, the boats and the coniferous 'bookend'. This leaves only the top of the frame for an arbitrary decision, but an amount of sky roughly equal to the height of the Granary and rather more than the mast of the Neljan (the large Dutch barge so often moored by the Quay) looked both appropriate and comfortable, so I settled for that.

The picture itself was completed very quickly in August 1993 and was an instant success. Within a month a run of four hundred limited edition prints was on sale followed later by two thousand greeting cards which have been reprinted several times.

What, I wondered, lay behind this success? In order to find some answers I took a ruler and black pen to one of the prints to make an analysis of the composition.

The centrality of the line of boats and the river bank on the right was of course obvious and so too was that of the sharp bend in the river bank below the end of the Granary and enclosing the reflection of the Mill in the remains of the last tide.

Next I measured out the vertical and horizontal Golden Means which play just as an important part in a two dimensional picture as they do on the fronts of the buildings themselves. And yes, the angle of the west end of the Mill and the fire escape ladder here straightaway proves the value in visual terms of the principle of the Golden Mean breaking the huge expanse of white weatherboarding. The man in the nearest boat stands resolutely on this vertical Golden Mean and so too does the central hoist on the front of the Granary more or less, together with the bow of the farthest of the boats moored against the Quay. The tallest mast – that of the Neljan – is also almost exactly on this division too.

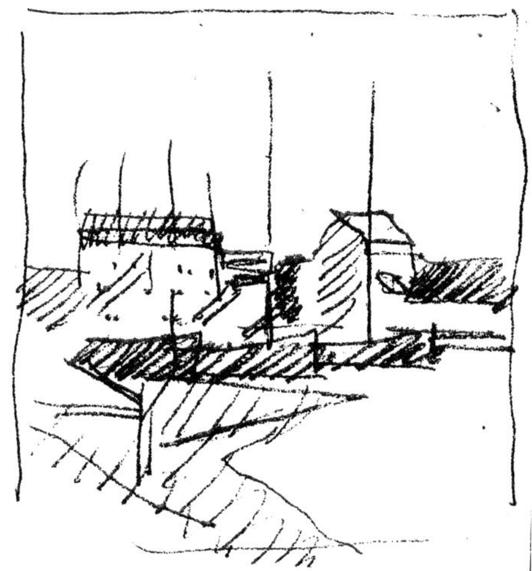

Sketch for another potential composition of this scene, not unlike the cover.

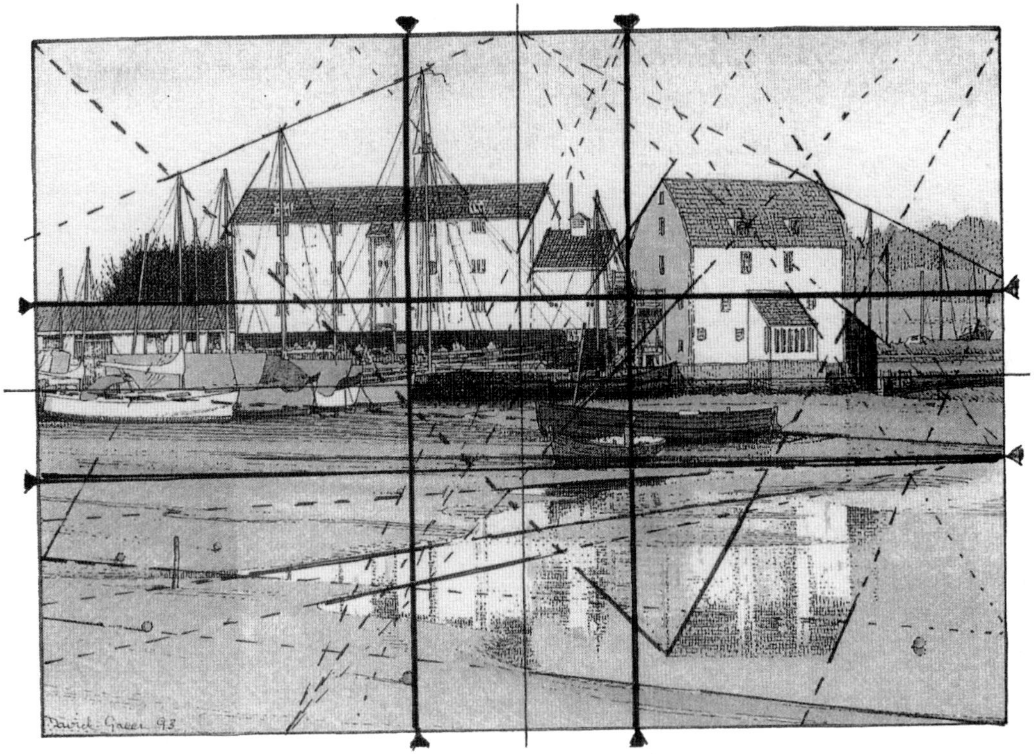

Compositional analysis of Plate One

The roof of the Art Club building sits exactly on the upper horizontal Golden Mean, but, more importantly, the green boat with the standing figure is situated directly on this lower Golden Mean where no less than five important lines in the mud, including three striking lengths of the water's edge, radiate directly from the right hand side of the picture at this point on the lower mean. These radiating lines should be ruled in right across a tracing or photocopy of the picture since our eyes follow straight lines unconsciously across gaps and out as far as the frame surrounding a picture.

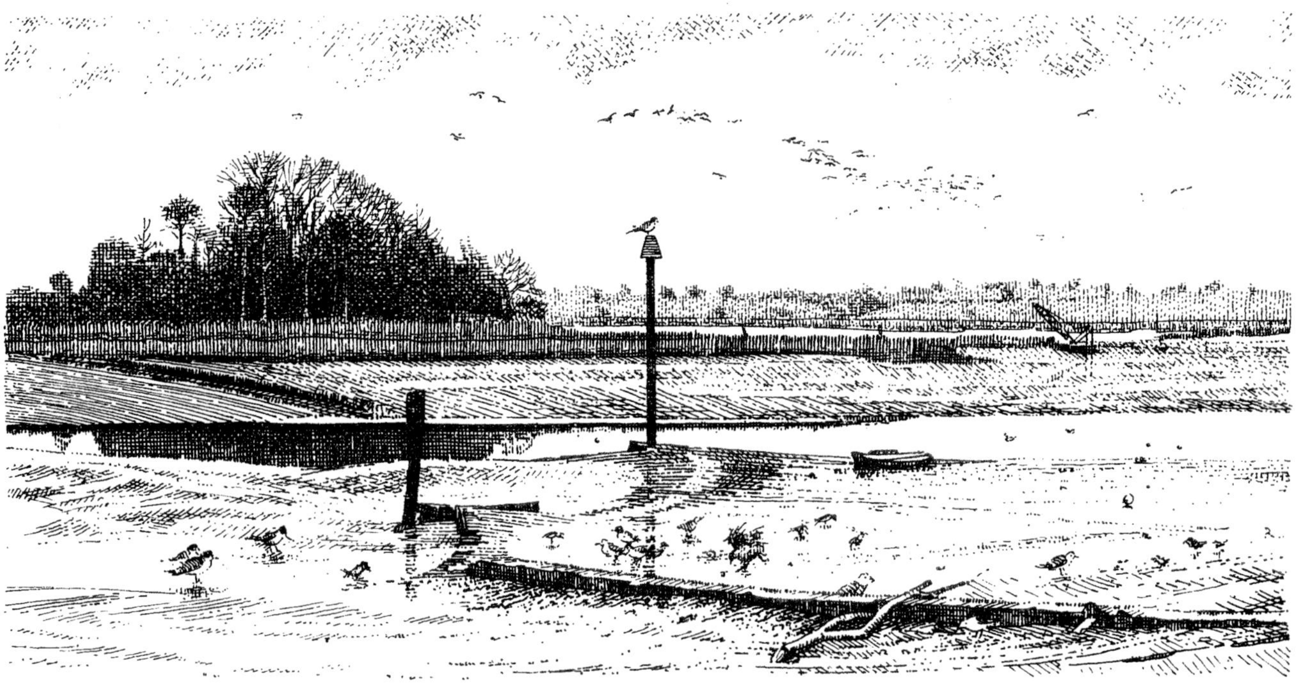

From the Quayside

At the frame these lines very often lead us back into the picture, sometimes bouncing our vision back and forth from side to side as indeed happens here with the line from the farthest penetration of the water which so startlingly reflects the front of the Granary. The line of this intrusion of the tide meets the frame on the left at exactly the point from where it is swept back across the scene to that edge of the mud which initially provided the clue for the placing of the right hand bottom corner of the frame. This is a very important link.

The search for connections and the abstract geometry that emanates, unconsciously from a picture that anyone bothers to look at a second time, leads us now to four particularly significant lines. Firstly, place your ruler across the tops of the tallest masts on either side of the buildings and you will find that the lines ruled across them will meet at exactly the top of the picture, confirming the position of the top edge chosen when the work began. And they meet exactly at the centre creating the suggestion of an arch over the top of the picture.

Then lastly look at the reflections of the roof of the Mill which is by far the most significant shape in this lower half of the picture and find out by ruling where the lines of the gable of the west end connect with the frame. Goodness, they have led us to the two top corners so that my hunch for the placing of the top of the frame and the positions of the two sides is confirmed again!

* * * * *

Plate Three TIDE MILL: MORNING (overleaf) is a splendid instance of the rotation of the sunlight mentioned earlier. I find particularly pleasing the two pointed fingers of light on the end of the Granary and the one on the Cottage which so satisfactorily terminates the shadow area and the gentle light that slightly illuminates the stern of the Neljan and the Quayside platform. The Tide Mill is also benefitting here from the strong triangular area of shadow caused by the sun lounge.

The viewpoint appears to be exactly the same as that of *Plate One THE GRANARY, THE COTTAGE AND THE TIDE MILL*, but substantial changes are made in the scene not only by the shadow on the Granary and the Cottage, but also the subtlety of light falling on the boats. Without the white tarpaulin beneath the Granary

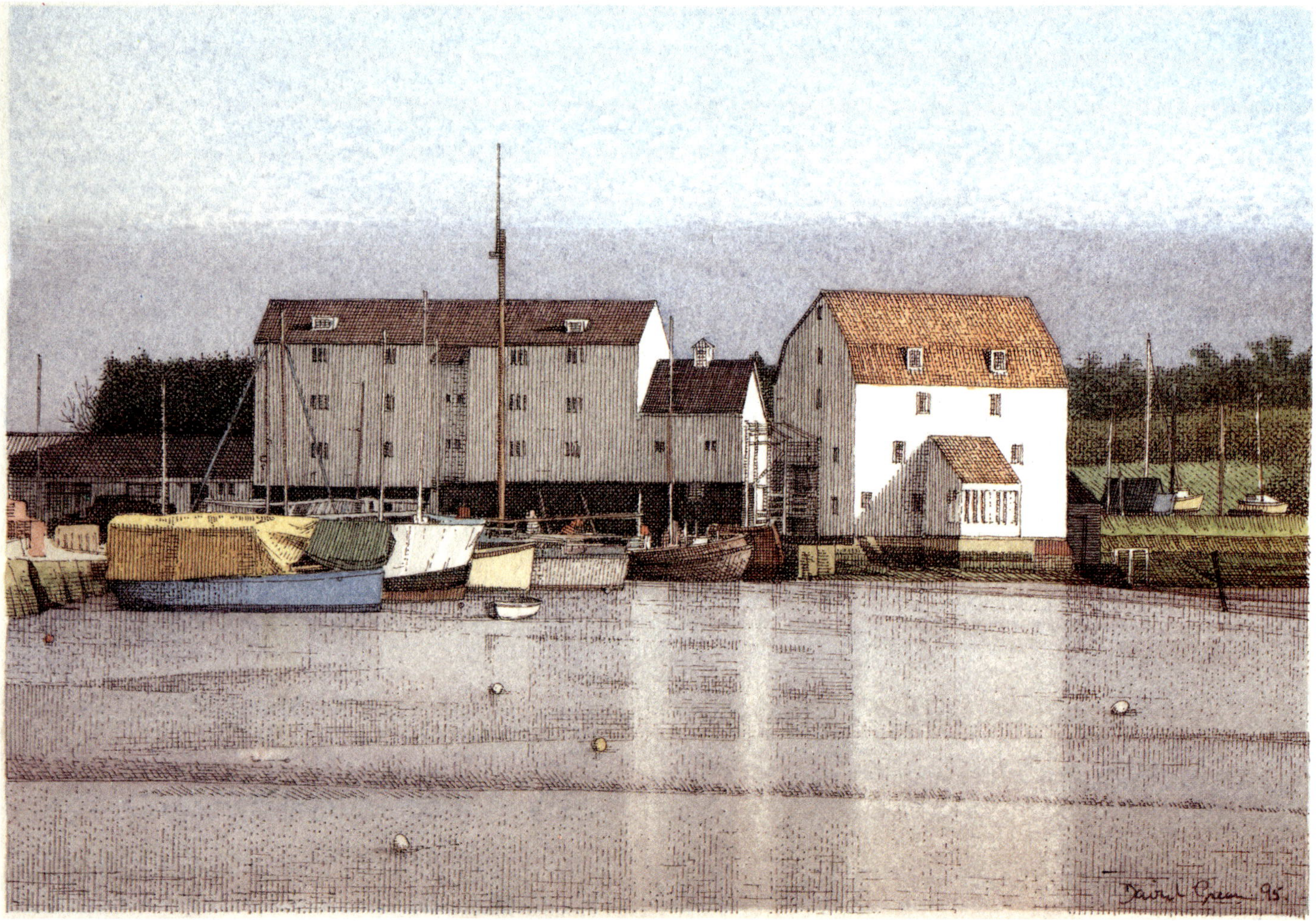

Plate Three *TIDE MILL: MORNING*

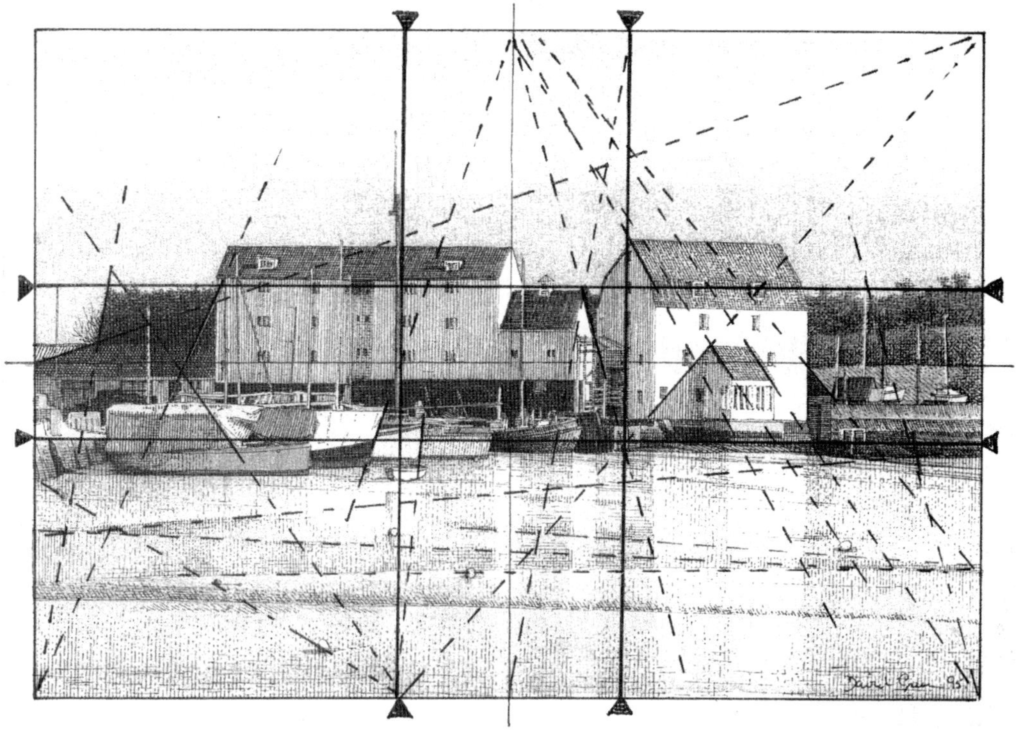

Compositional Analysis of Plate Three

and the play of light across the cover on the nearest boat, there would have been no vibes to cause me to stop on my walk along the river path to the town and no picture either. The white tarpaulin is beautifully placed away from the other sunlit areas of the Mill and the colours of the nearest boat – blue, yellow and a quiet green – are most pleasing additions to the scene. The light upon the boats in the landscape on the right is beneficial too. And notice the triangle of sunlight on the roof of the Art Club on the left which firmly directs our vision across the picture to the far top right corner.

Leaving aside any further details of *Plate Three,* there is a strong horizontal element in this picture caused by the mud and the cloud banks that sit behind the buildings which suffuse a calm and delightful peace over the scene, enhanced by the subtly contrasting verticals of the reflected lights.

Plate Five. SNOW. The Granary and Tide Mill in Snow seems crazy. Everything is wrong. We do not have snow in Woodbridge – at least not more than about once in a decade. The snow covered mud is so bright that it almost hurts the eyes; so too are the roofs. The weatherboarding which is usually bright is dull; the sky is dark; the black crane has replaced the Art Club and the line of tarpaulin covered boats has been replaced by the jetty. The dominant feature of the composition is no longer the Tide Mill – it is now just a wall of breeze blocks. All perfectly true and yet curiously exciting for it reminds us that, in a picture, all that really matters are the shapes and colours of the objects depicted – and of course the way they fit together inside the frame!

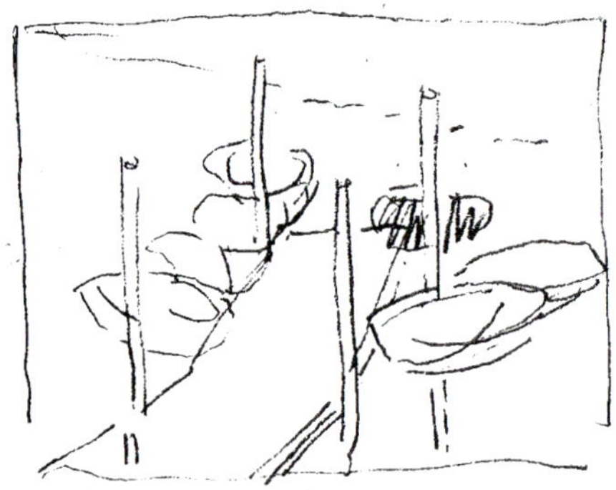

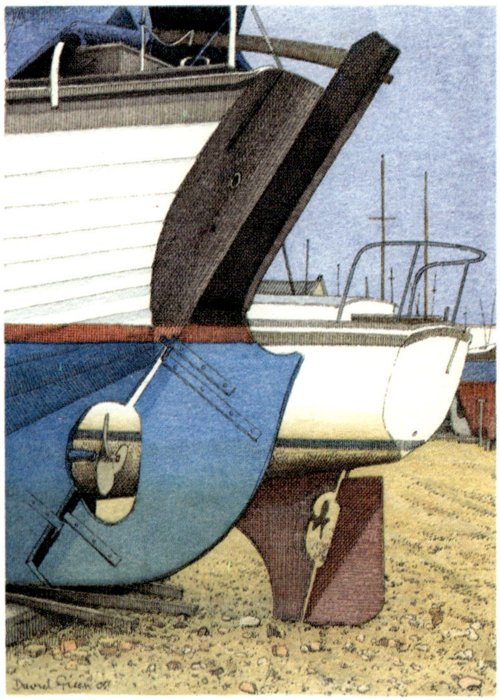

Plate Four.
SHAPES AND COLOURS FROM EVERSONS' BOATYARD and a scribble from the waterfront.

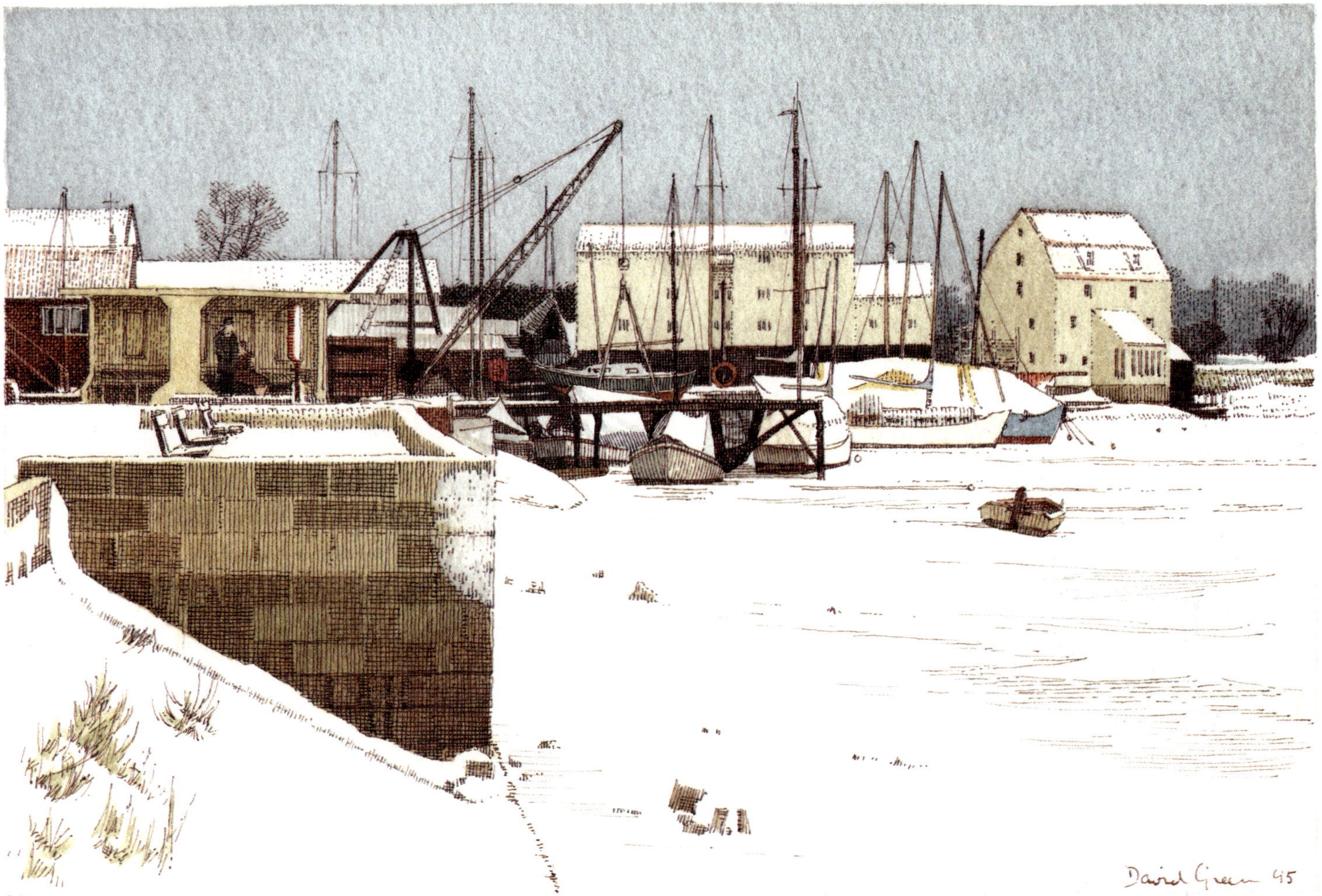

Plate Five. SNOW.

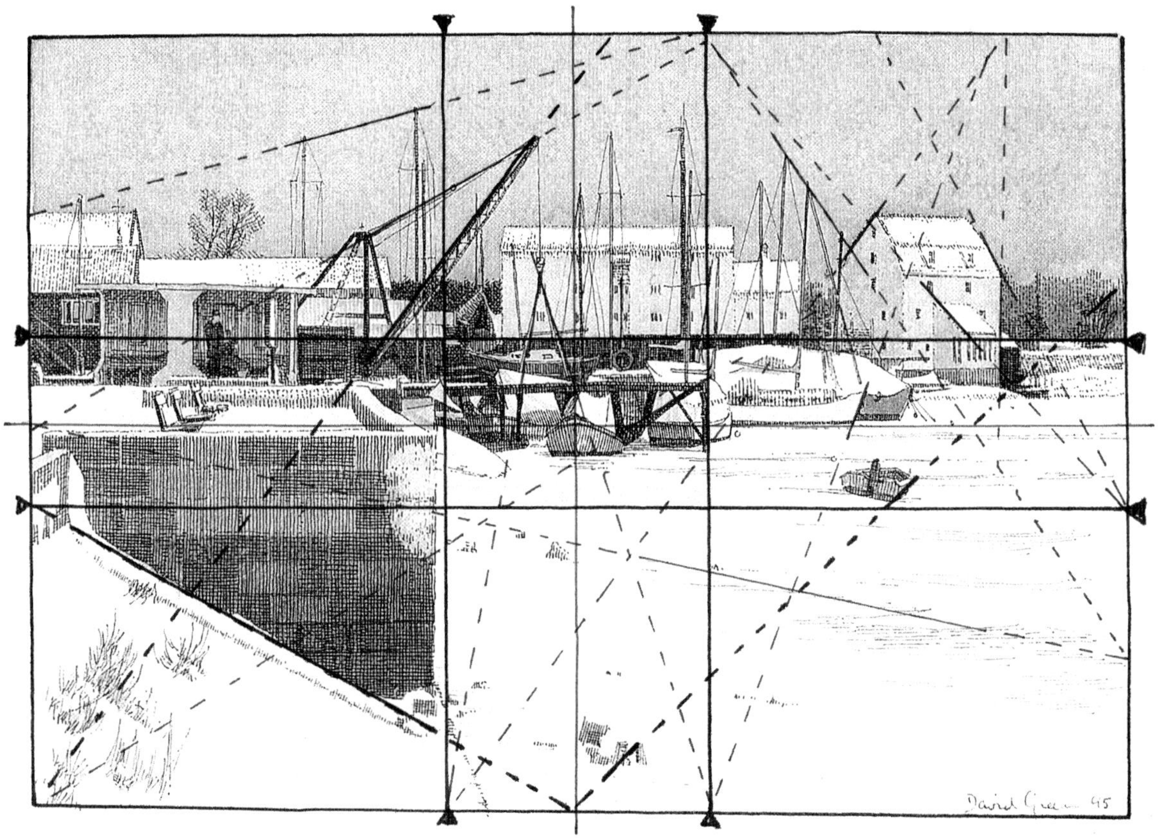

Compositional analysis of Plate Five

The breeze block wall is in fact an interesting shape fitting exactly the space below the centre line and beside the left hand Golden Mean. It is subdivided by a pattern of different blocks filling the space down as far as the lower Mean, while the base line of the triangle leads our eyes to the centre at the bottom. Its bold richly coloured shapes contrast nicely with the decidedly busy line of crane, jetty, boats and buildings which stretches right across the picture until it meets the 'book end' of the wheel house on the Mill which is incidentally a chief motivating factor of the Mill despite its insignificance.

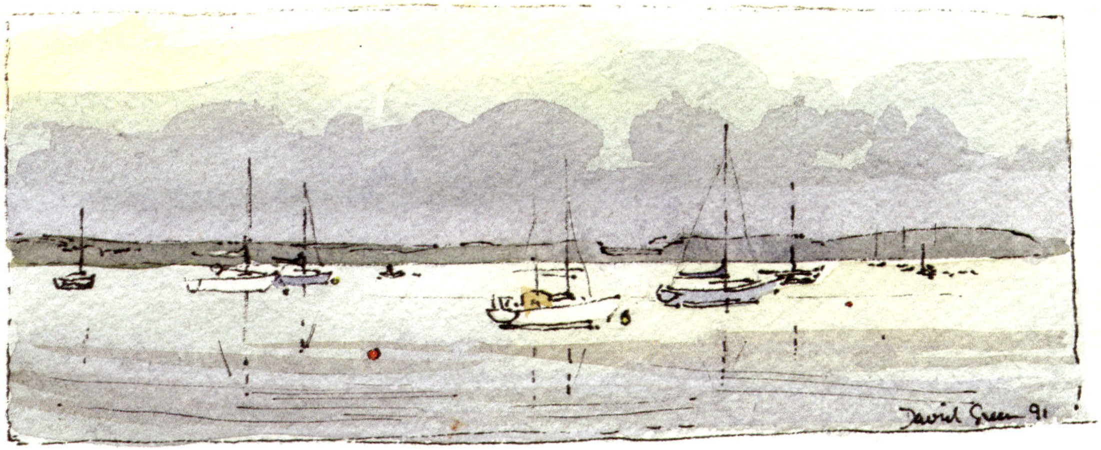

Plate Six. ON THE DEBEN (A Sketch)

The gib of the crane follows a line from near the top centre down to the left hand corner of the composition and the triangular shapes are echoed in the crane and the busy pattern of the dark jetty timbers.

The jetty itself fits neatly between the two Golden Means occupying the central area between the breeze blocks and the more open space up as far as the right hand edge. In this space the isolated boat sits on a line between some discarded bricks at the bottom and the dark shape of the wheelhouse, keeping our eyes focussed firmly inside the important areas of the picture.

Few readers who are not painters themselves will perhaps readily appreciate that the substance of these analyses of the picture reproduced in *PLATES ONE to THREE* is as new to me as it may be to them, since these analyses were made especially for these pages more or less twenty years after the pictures had been painted. They are *afterthoughts* rather than *forethoughts* and the pictures themselves were the results of intuition, inspiration, perception and solid experience coupled with the sort of visual excitement described earlier.

Constable is a helpful example for us from the professional world of picture making back in history. His major works – the larger ones submitted to the annual Summer Exhibition at the Royal Academy – reveal an astonishing air of conviction and timeless reality which might appear to have no need for the support of any detailed framework of abstract compositional geometry, but this is the opposite of the truth. The Cornfield in the National Gallery has been the subject of any number of investigations over the years, always with the same result. The picture is firmly held together by a rigid abstract framework starting from the positioning of the chief visual features – the cornfield itself and the major tree on the left – set squarely upon the Golden Means.

Following on from the positioning of these two major features are four significant focal points on the frame as shown on the diagram opposite and many other lines radiating from the white spot on the dog's nose which is often thought of as a key point in this composition.

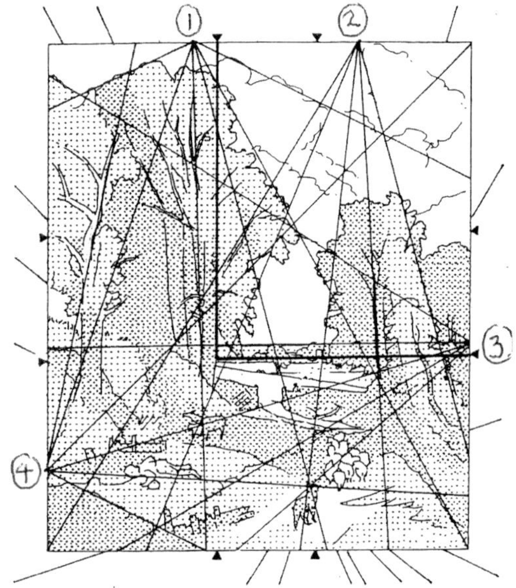

Compositional analysis of Constable's Cornfield painted in 1826, 56¼ x 48 inches (1430 x 1220 cm). The picture is in the National Gallery.

But, in spite of all this linear structure there is no evidence anywhere of Constable ruling lines for compositional purposes on this or any others of his work. The Cornfield is the result of months of intuitive work, pacing back and forth to assess the placing of virtually every brush stroke from a distance where it could be seen in relation to the rest. He wrote of this period whilst he was engaged upon this picture:-

> *My picture occupied me wholly: I could think of and speak to no one. I felt like a relation of mine at the battle of Waterloo. He said he dare not turn his head right or left, but always kept it straight forward, thinking of himself alone!...*

I have never lived with a Constable, other than an odd card or reproduction, to test fully his sensitivity, but here in the studio where I work is a print of an etching (see over) by John Sell Cotman, another recognised master of the East Anglian School of painters which I had bought some fifty years ago and which now hangs opposite my desk. It has not the scale of a Constable, or the colour of course, but the geometry is there as you can see in the diagram and it holds the attention. One's eyes are led back and forth across its surface time and again and always with the same level of enchantment.

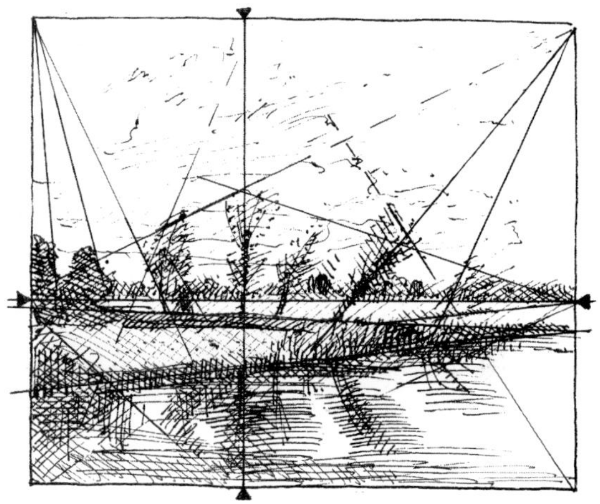

Compositional sketch of a smaller picture by Constable - The Water Meadows at Salisbury - which may have been painted partly on the spot. The picture is in the Victoria and Albert Museum.

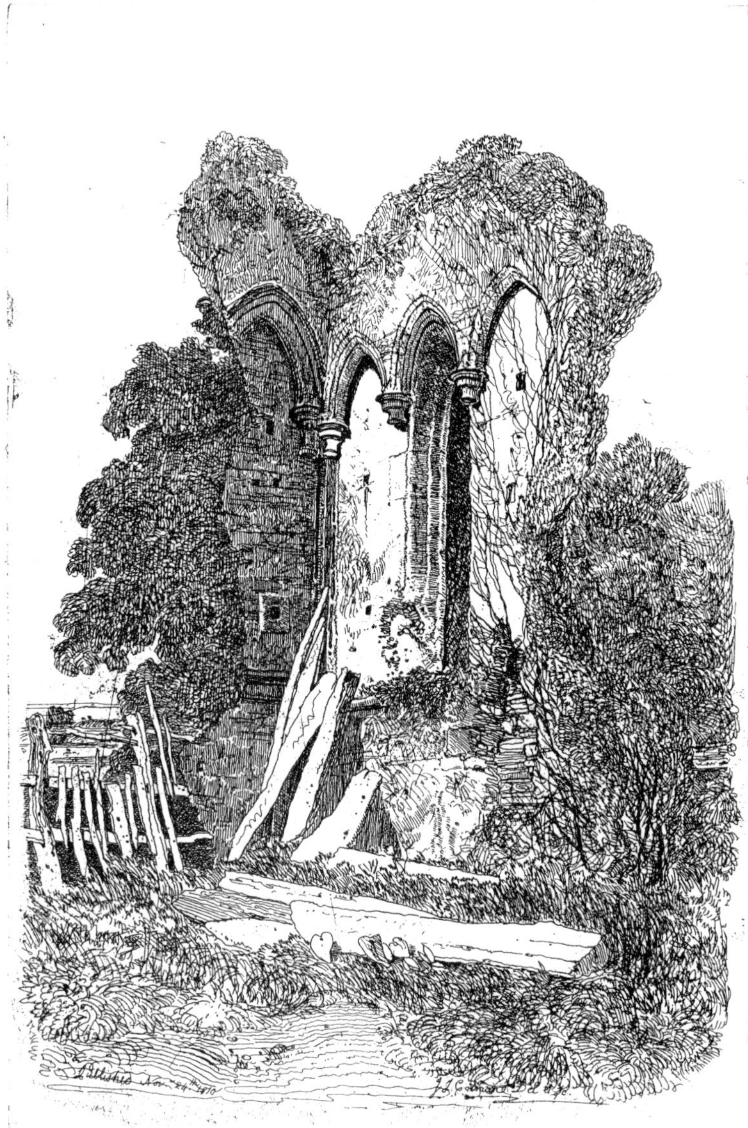

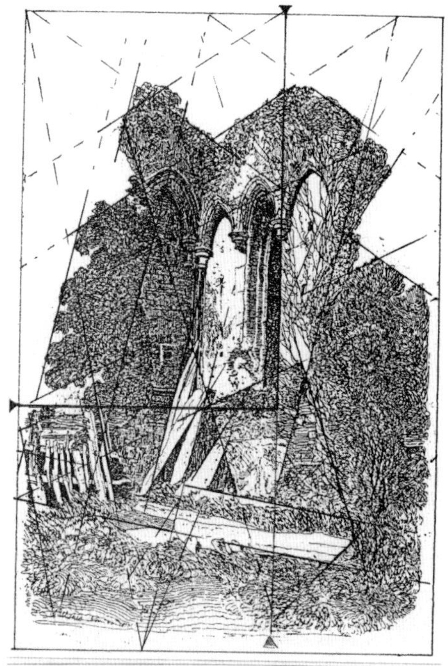

ETCHING BY
JOHN SELL COTMAN.
1810

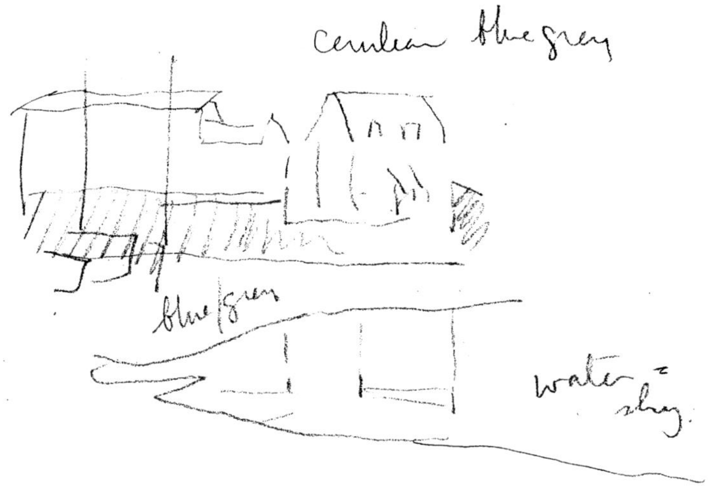

The illustrations in this last section, some very sketchy indeed, are important to me as reminders of views that looked as though they had potential for making pictures and would be worth looking at again. That on the left is from that point on the river path where "the breath left my body in one gasp". It is the briefest of sketches and not much of a note. It is a WHOOPEE - GET BACK AS QUICK AS YOU CAN for it contains just the purest essence of *Plate One*, the remains of the tide, the reflection, a hint of the masts and the briefest indications of colours – "water = sky"! I was back as soon as I could get there and in the meantime the boats had arrived on the mudbank which enhanced the composition. Photographs were taken there and then for structural details and several interesting oddments were observed – the light on the fire escape for instance – which filled out the essence.

Overleaf there is additional information concerning the range of tonal values in a scene recorded on a numerical scale from 1 to 7, as well as a summary of the colours in addition to the sky – white, purple, orange and black. Much the same as *Plate One* though you may notice an important hint about the sky greying low down.

However it is the numerical scale of tones we need to look at first. Tones are not colours though the same word is often used because the two are to some extent interdependent. They are degrees of light to dark which would hopefully show in black and white photographs, though they rarely reveal themselves accurately in this medium because each colour affects the film – or the digits! - differently.

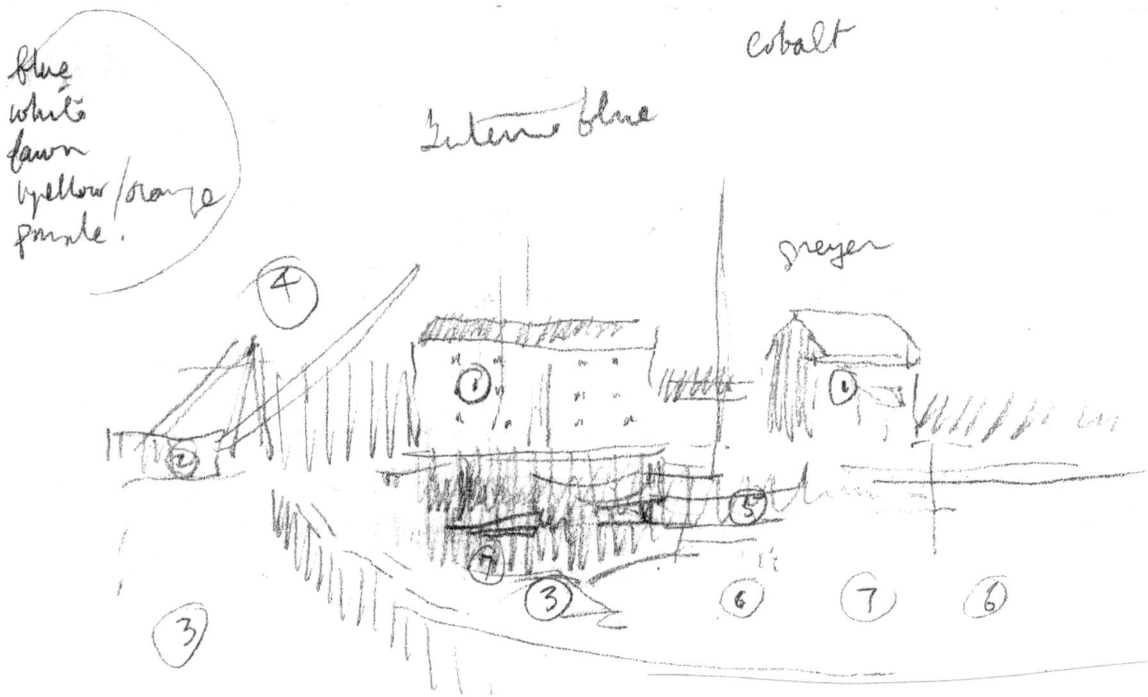

Tonal Notes

Only rarely is anyone able to distinguish more than seven or eight different tonal values in a scene, but if this range is truthfully observed from corner to corner, from top to bottom and side to side – and accurately recorded in paint – the result will be astonishing. It will have a sparkling freshness with conviction and depth which, as Sir Kenneth Clarke once noted, will "strike you with the same physical sensation as a singer with a perfect sense of pitch".

And unusually such accuracy of vision cannot be achieved by opening the eyes wider to the subject. Rather the reverse, almost closing them is the answer. As the lids are drawn together, the details and all the fussy complexities fuse together leaving only the basic shapes to be assessed.

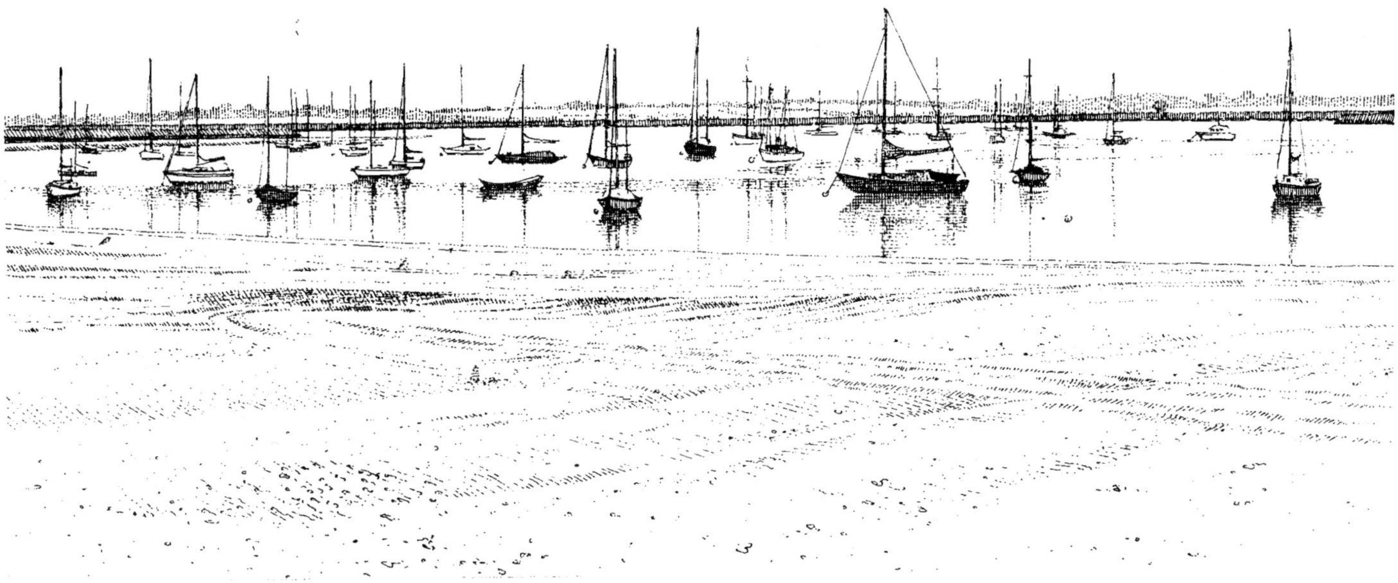

To the South

So, in creating a picture in this traditional *perceptual* manner there are three distinct areas to be looked at. First the shapes and lines which make up the pattern and contain the abstract geometry or the vibes that initially aroused our visual interest; secondly the tonal scale which secures solidity and conviction and, thirdly, the colours which are not always necessary since the tones on their own, in shades of grey or sepia pigments, can make powerful and convincing 'monochrome' images.

All this information can be sorted and settled most surely and convincingly in the mind by talking to oneself as one's eyes wander back and forth across the subject. Words are solid and the effort to find the right ones to describe what one sees enhances both memory and perception.

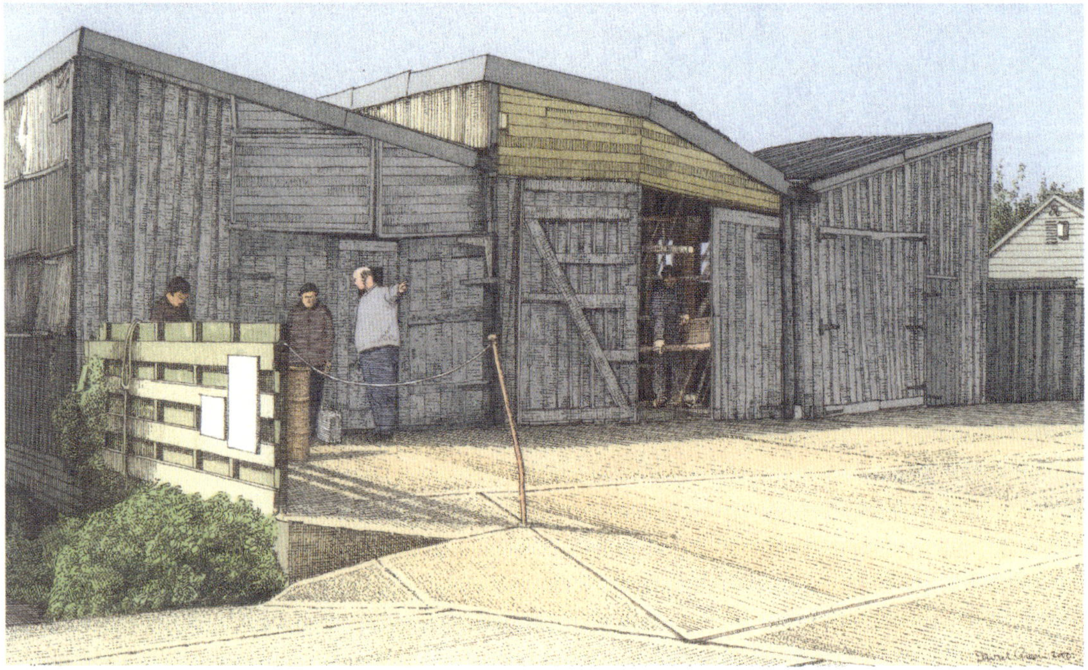

Plate Seven.   EVERSONS' BOATSHED.

DOWN RIVER

Time now to take a walk and to enjoy some of the scenery that lies between the Mill and Kyson Point which is the farthest you can proceed southwards (about a mile as the crow flies) without being forced to turn inland.

However, before we leave the waterfront in the town Eversons' shed deserves attention since it provides the perfect counter to the neat formality of the Quay complex. It is by far the wackiest building we shall see here and one can only conclude that it grew on the site because it is impossible to imagine it ever having evolved from drawings on an architect's board!

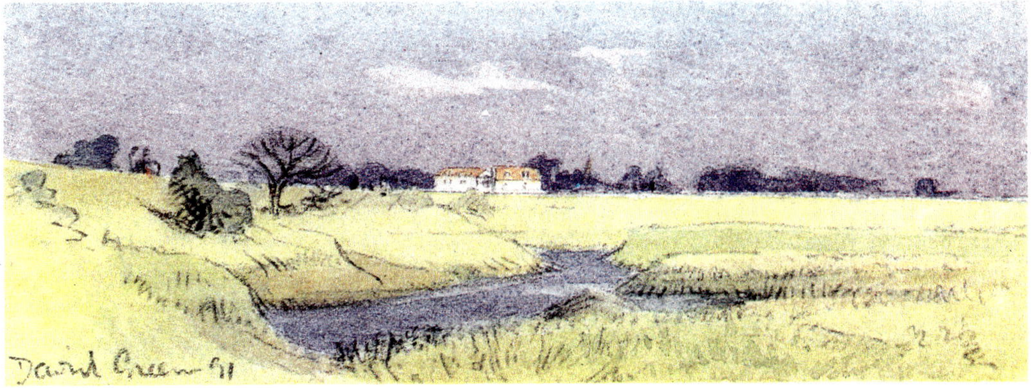

Plate Eight. LOOKING NORTH FROM KYSON

The building is sometimes referred to locally as the Phoenix Works because it was rebuilt after a fire between the wars using much of the original timber. They say too that it lay flat to allow the Hurricane of 1987 to pass over it without doing any damage and more recently it has survived a 'restoration' when the attractive vertical grey painted weatherboards shown in *Plate Seven* were replaced by thinner ones laid horizontally and treated only with wood preserver. Is it not time for a Preservation Order?

After leaving Eversons' the path to Kyson has been carefully built up to protect Woodbridge from the encroachment of the sea and it now provides a splendid walk with uninterrupted views of the River Deben, the estuary, the unique bird life and the ever changing conditions of the sky. It is the loveliest route one can imagine.

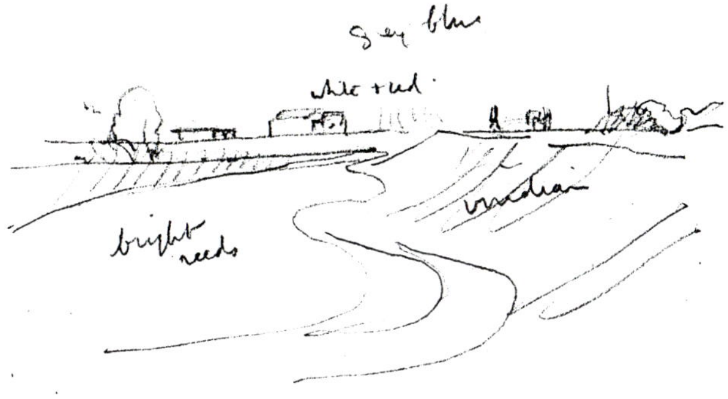

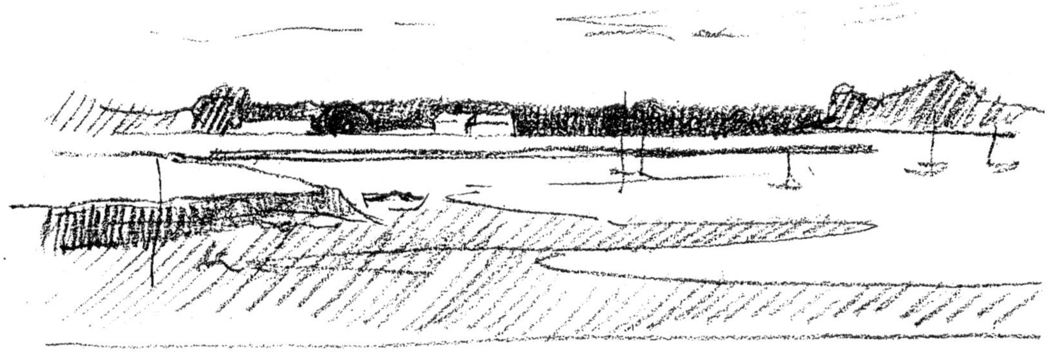

FROM NEAR THE YACHT CLUB

As you approach Kyson Point the path turns sharply to the left through trees and descends to a short length of beach which is sometimes impassable at high tide and from which my drawing opposite was made a year or two after the Hurricane. There was still plenty of dereliction about, although the worst damage was four or five miles to the north around Rendlesham where several whole forests were torn down in a matter of seconds.

On the return walk the Mill and the Granary come back into view almost immediately and shine in the sunlight like jewels.

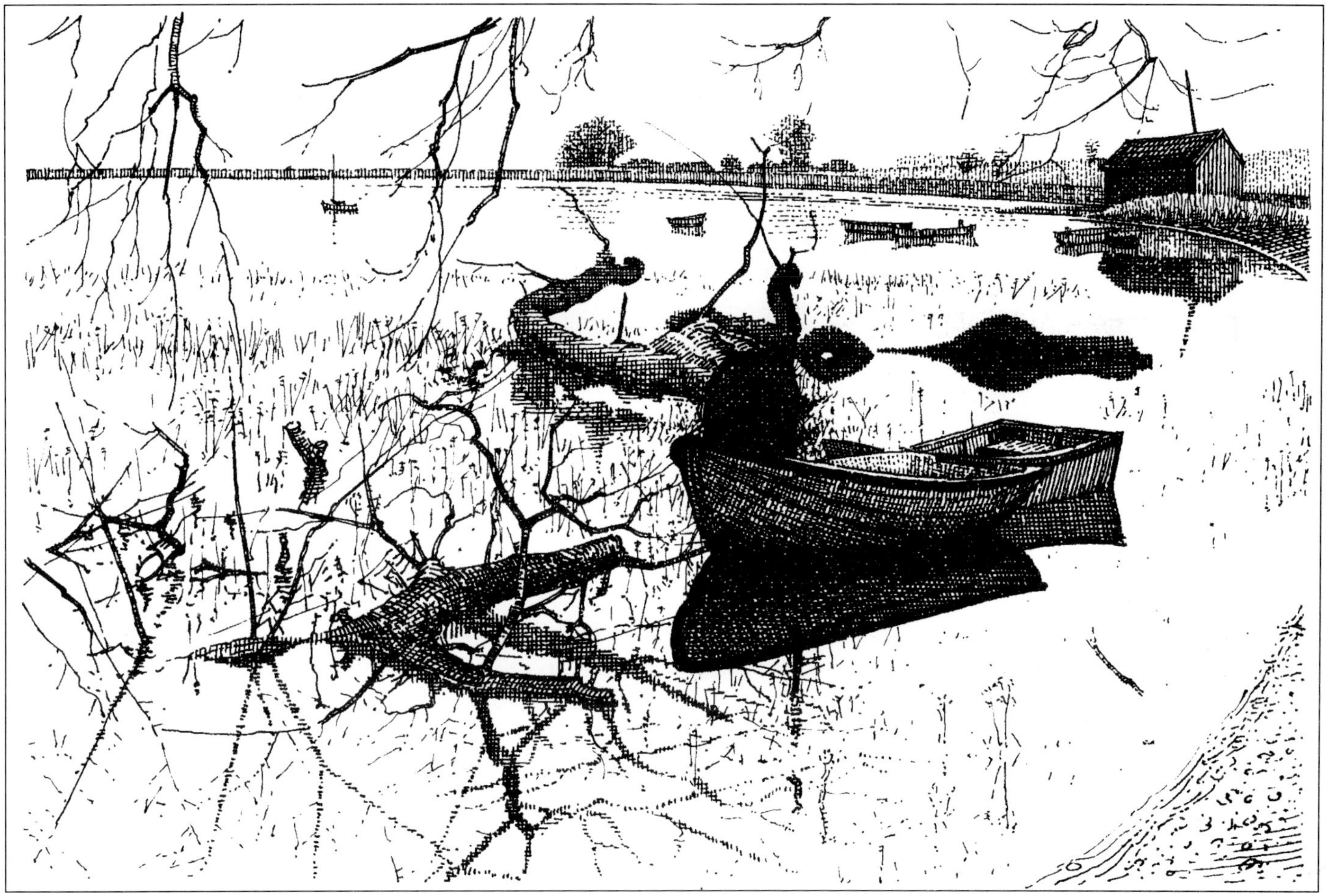

KYSON CREEK A YEAR OR SO AFTER THE HURRICANE.

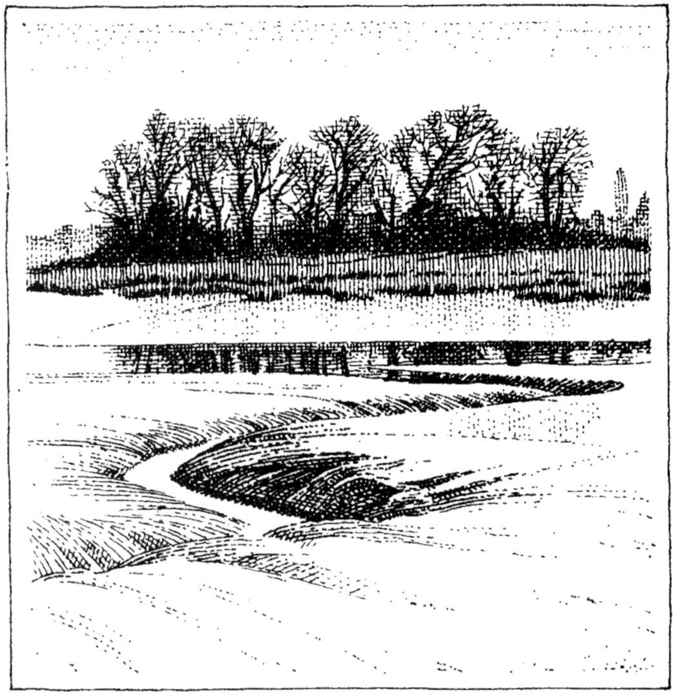

KYSON CREEK

However, an immediate return is not the only option because from the far end of Kyson Beach up towards the boating hut on the right hand side of the drawing on the previous page there is a narrow path that turns inland and leads one along the bank of Martlesham Creek which has its own special beauty and adds a further worthwhile mile or so to the walk.